W9-CEI-405

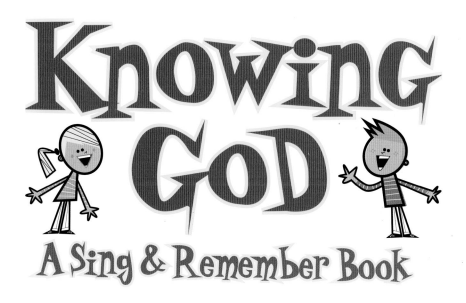

Knowing God

A Sing & Remember Book

Created by
Stephen Elkins

Illustrations by
David Semple

INTEGRITY®
PUBLISHERS
family
Nashville

About the Author: S T E P H E N   E L K I N S is one of America's foremost children's writers whose work has sold over 5 million children's books and CD's. He has received numerous awards including a nomination for the prestigious GRAMMY AWARD. Stephen has over 300 books, audio productions and DVD's to his credit including *The Memory Bible, The LullaBible* and *The Word & Song Bible.* Owner of Wonder Workshop, which is reported to be the 5th largest independent children's production company in the world (*BillBoard Magazine*), his books and children's Bibles remain at the top of the Best-Sellers list, as well as The Wonder Kids Choir recordings which maintained over 100 consecutive weeks on *BillBoard's* Top Kid Audio Chart in 2003. Stephen's workshops on music and Scripture Memory for Children continue to be very successful. Stephen lives in Nashville with his wife Cindy and their three children.

K N O W I N G   G O D
A Sing & Remember Book

Stories and songs written by Stephen Elkins.

Published by Integrity Publishers, a division of Integrity Media, Inc., 5250 Virginia Way, Suite 110, Brentwood, TN 37027.

www.integritypublishers.com

I N T E G R I T Y   P U B L I S H E R S ,   I N C .
H E L P I N G   P E O P L E   W O R L D W I D E   E X P E R I E N C E   *the*   M A N I F E S T   P R E S E N C E   *of*   G O D

Illustrated by David Semple

Cover and interior design: Russ McIntosh, Mark Mickel, Brand Navigation, LLC—www.brandnavigation.com

Special thanks to: The Wonder Kids Choir: Emily Elkins, Laurie Harper, Audrey Hollifield, Amy Lawrence, Lindsey McAdams, Amy McPeak, and Allie Smith.

Engineer: Randy Moore

Arrangements: John DeVries

Library of Congress Cataloging-in-Publication Data
ISBN: 1-59145-432-8

Printed in China

06 07 08 09 RRD 9 8 7 6 5 4 3 2 1

TABLE OF CONTENTS

GOD is The CreaToR

MY MEMORY verse

God CREATED the heavens and the earth.

Genesis 1:1

THINKIN' 2day

It's really fun to make things

with your own hands.

With a little glue and an hour

or two, you can make almost anything.

You and Mom can make a kite out of paper and string.

You can help Dad make a birdhouse

out of wood and nails.

But do you know what God made?

The Creation Story

(Day 1)

God made the heavens and the earth with only His words. He spoke, and the heavens came to be. He spoke again, and the earth was made. He used no paper or string, no wood or nails. In fact, He used nothing at all. He is so powerful and creative that He made everything with only His words!

You can read
this story in the
Book of Genesis,
chapters 1 and 2!

3

The Bible says that God created
the heavens and the earth.
It also says God created *you*. It says that
He knew you before you were even born.
And all that God creates is good.
Thank You God for this wonderful world
You have created.

for me today!

let's sing!

God Created

<u>Chorus</u>
In the beginning! Oh, in the beginning!
In the beginning,
God created the heavens and the earth.
In the beginning,
God created the heavens and the earth,
The heavens and the earth.

He is so mighty, we sing,
In the beginning! Oh, in the beginning!
With only words,
He created every living thing.
So lift your voices and sing!

(Repeat chorus)

We sing the glory of God.
In the beginning! Oh, in the beginning!
We praise His name!
Lift Him high above creation
Because He created it all!

4

God Our Maker

So God created man in his own image.

Genesis 1:27

Do you remember a time when the circus came to town? Did you go into the house of mirrors? You probably couldn't believe how funny it made you look! In one mirror, you looked short and fat.

In another, you appeared to be tall and skinny. Your image would change with every mirror. It would be easy to forget what you really looked like!

Adam and Eve

(Day 6)

Bible
Story

God made human beings in His own image.
Adam and Eve were perfect in every way. God put them in
the Garden of Eden where they would have everything
they needed. God blessed them and said,
"Have many children and grow in number.
Fill the earth and be its master . . . Rule over every living
thing that moves on the earth" (Genesis 1:28 ICB).

Then God said it was very good!

You can read
the whole story
in Genesis,
chapter 1!

Some people have forgotten what they are supposed to look like on the inside. They were created in the image of God. Yet because of their sinful habits, it's hard to see God in them.

God is joyful and loving. You should be too!

God is honest and trustworthy. You should be too! God is faithful and just. Yes—you should be too! This world can bend your image like a house of mirrors. But don't forget— you were made in the image of God!

for me today!

let's sing!

In His Own Image

Chorus
God created, so God created,
God created, so God created,
God created man in His own image, oh, yeah!

We know God made the heavens.
We know God made the earth.
We know God made the oceans.
He made the beautiful surf.
We know God made a woman.
We know God made a man.
We know He created them in His image.
Please understand.

(Repeat chorus)

We know God made the mountains.
We know God made the seas.
We know God made the deserts.
He made the beautiful trees.
We know God made a woman.
We know God made a man.
We know He created them in His image.
Please understand.

(Repeat chorus)

God is All-Powerful

MY MEMORY verse

"What is impossible with men is possible with God."
Luke 18:27

THINKIN' 2day

The doctors came out of the operating room with their heads lowered. They had worked very hard to remove the cancer. The family walked quietly into the hospital room and knelt beside little Zach's bed to pray. "Lord, the doctors said only a miracle can heal him now. We know You are all-powerful. So do what is impossible for us to do." The Lord answered their prayers, and Zach got well.

God can do all things!

Abraham & Sarah Receive a Miracle

(Around 2066 B.C.)

Bible Story

Sarah actually experienced God's power! She was the wife of Abraham. God had promised them a son. He told Abraham that his descendants would outnumber the stars in the sky. But many years had passed and Abraham was now 100 years old. When the Lord told Abraham it was time to have a son, Sarah laughed. "God can't do that," she thought. "We're too old!" But, one year later, a little baby named Issac was born. Sarah knew that God could go all things! His power was great!

Is anything too hard for the Lord?

Whether it's healing the sick or

keeping His promise that a baby will be born,

God can do it! Let these words

encourage you: your God can!

He can do what no man can do.

All things are possible in the hands of almighty God.

let's sing!

What Is Impossible with Men

Chorus
What is impossible with men,
Is possible with God!
No matter what the odds may be,
In Christ I find my victory!
What is impossible with men,
Is possible with God, my friend!
Through it all, come thick or thin,
I'll believe, it's possible with Him.

Too hard? Nothing can be
Too hard if you believe.
God will answer me,
If I pray and I believe.

(Repeat chorus)

Too big? Is anything
Too big for Jesus our King?
Nothing He cannot do,
Just believe, God's Word is true.

(Repeat chorus)

GOD is Awesome

HOW AWESOME is the LORD Most High.

Psalm 47:2

Lots of days are very *good.* A day full of sunny, blue skies is a very good day. Other days can be *great.* A day at the beach, flying kites with your friends is a *great* day. But every now and then, you have a really awesome day.

An *awesome* day is better than good. It's even greater than great. It's the very best day of all!

Moses Parts the Red Sea

(Around 1446 B.C.)

Once, Moses and the people

of Israel had a really awesome day.

They were about to be attacked by the Egyptian army.

With the desert  in front of them and the Red Sea

behind them, there was no way of escape.

But God is an awesome God. He parted the Red Sea,

and God's people walked to safety!

What an awesome day!

You can read the whole story in the Book of Exodus, chapter 14!

God is more than good.

God is greater than great.

God is awesome! The Bible says there

is none like Him. He is awesome because

He can do all things. There is no problem too big

for God. He can solve any problem, even if He

has to part a sea! Got a little problem? Got a giant problem?

Remember, God is better than good, greater than great.

God is an awesome God!

for me today!

let's sing!

How Awesome Is the Lord

Chorus
How awesome, how awesome is the Lord our God!
He is good.
How awesome, how awesome is our God!
He is an awesome God!

More than good, greater than great,
Our God is an awesome God!
He can part a sea, defeat an enemy.
Our God is an awesome God!
Oh, our God is an awesome God!

(Repeat chorus)

More than good, greater than great,
No problem too big for Him.
Oh, His mighty hand no evil can withstand.
Our God is an awesome God!
Oh, our God is an awesome God!

(Repeat chorus)

**"For my thoughts are not
your thoughts, neither are
your ways my ways,"
declares the LORD.**
Isaiah 55:8

"Hiccup!" *What do I have to do to make these things*

go away? Michael wondered. He walked over to Dad,

opened his mouth to speak, and—"Hiccup!"

With a grin, Dad instructed, "Hold your breath

and swallow ten times." Michael gave him a funny

look, but unable to question him—"Hiccup!"—Michael

tried it. And what do you know? The hiccups went away!

How did he know what to do?

17

Joshua and the Battle of Jericho

(Around 1400 B.C.)

Joshua's army crossed the Jordan River into the

Promised Land. There, they would battle the Canaanites

at Jericho. But the Lord told Joshua to do a

very strange thing. To win the battle, the Lord told him

to march around the walls of Jericho once a day

for six days. Then, on the seventh day, march again,

sound the trumpets, and shout!

Even though it sounded strange,

Joshua obeyed the Lord.

The walls of Jericho fell exactly like the Lord said they would!

God knew exactly what to do.

19

What a strange way to win a battle! Joshua's army didn't use their strength. They didn't use their weapons. They didn't need to.

They simply obeyed God's command. God's ways are not your ways. Sometimes He does things a little differently than you might do them. But no matter what today may bring, you must be of good courage like Joshua. And you must trust your heavenly Father.

He always knows the best way!

My Thoughts Are Not Your Thoughts

Chorus

"For My thoughts are not your thoughts,
Neither are your ways My ways,"
Declares the Lord to all who will believe.
"For My thoughts are not your thoughts,
Neither are your ways My ways,"
Declares the Lord to all who will believe.

Do you believe in the Lord who is almighty?
Yes, we do!
Have courage and wait upon the Lord.
Do you believe in the Lord who is almighty?
Alrighty then!
Have courage, wait upon the Lord!

(Repeat chorus)

Do you believe in the Lord who's always listening?
Yes, we do!
Have courage and call upon the Lord.
Do you believe in the Lord who's always listening?
I'm insisting!
Have courage, wait upon the Lord!

(Repeat chorus)

God Answers Prayers

In the morning, O LORD, you hear my voice.

Psalm 5:3

THINKIN'
2day

Katy had just woke up from the scariest nightmare! She sat straight up in her bed and looked around in the darkness. "Mom?" she called in a meek voice. In seconds, Mom stood at her doorway, turned on the light, and came to Katy's side to comfort her. "I'm here. It's all right," she whispered. Katy's mom was right there when Katy called, even in the wee hours of the morning.

Joshua Prays to God

(Around 1400 B.C.)

Bible Story

Joshua knew he could call on God at any time. When great forces stood against Joshua and his army, he prayed to God for help. God answered his prayer. He told Joshua, "Do not be afraid of them; I have given them into your hand" (Joshua 10:8). God confused the enemy, and Joshua and his men marched in and took them by surprise. With the power of God behind him, Joshua and his army defeated the mighty forces against them.

You can read the whole story in Joshua, chapter 10!

23

Many wake up each morning and never even think about the Lord. They go about their day with good health and blessings, never thinking of the One who has given it all to them. Let the Lord hear your voice. Let Him know you're thankful for all He's done in your life. When you get up and begin a new day, let God hear your voice, and take time to listen to His.

for me today!

let's sing!

You Hear My Voice

In the morning, Lord, You hear my voice.
In the morning, Lord, You hear me call.
In the morning, Lord, You hear my voice,
Praising who You are, saying,

Chorus
Holy, holy You are!
Worthy, worthy You are!
Honor we give to Your name!
Hear us Lord, our glad refrain!
Hear us Lord, our glad refrain!

At noontime, Lord, You hear my voice.
At noontime, Lord, You hear me call.
At noontime, Lord, You hear my voice,
Praising who You are, saying,

(Repeat chorus)

At bedtime, Lord, You hear my voice.
At bedtime, Lord, You hear me call.
At bedtime, Lord, You hear my voice,
Praising who You are, saying . . .

(Repeat chorus)

"I am the vine; you are the branches ... apart from me you can do nothing."

John 15:5

The thunder was getting louder and louder.

Suddenly, a bolt of lightning lit up the entire night sky.

Boom! went the thunder; then the lights went out.

"Turn on the lights!" cried Bobby, John's little four-year-old brother. "We didn't turn the lights off, Bobby," John's mom explained in a comforting voice.

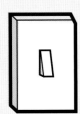

"When the electric power is off, the lights won't work."

Samson, the Strongest Man

(Around 1050 B.C.)

Samson's source of power and strength was the Lord. Before Samson was born, an angel came to Samson's mother. The angel told her that her baby would be blessed with the gift of strength in order to do God's work. The angel explained that Samson's hair was never to be cut. She followed the angel's instructions, and Samson soon grew to be the most powerful man in the world. He defeated over a thousand men using the jawbone of a donkey! Later, Samson fell in love with a woman named Delilah. Delilah didn't believe in God. When Samson told her the secret of his strength, she told his secret to the enemy. The enemy cut off his hair. He was powerless!

You can read
the whole story
in Judges,
chapters 13 to 16!

27

Your source of strength is the Lord.
He is like a vine that feeds all the branches.
The branches then feed the grapes.
If the grape is cut off from the vine,
it dies. Likewise, if you cut yourself
off from the Lord, you lose your source of strength.
You can do nothing. You are powerless like Samson. But, if
you stay attached to Jesus, you're like a lamp that has the
electricity on . . . you shine! You can do all things through
Christ who strengthens you.

for me today!

let's sing!

I Am the Vine

Chorus
I, I, I, I am the vine.
I, I, I, I am the vine.
You, you, you, you are the branches.
But I, I, I, I am the vine.
Apart from Me you can do nothing.
Apart, you see, you can do nothing.
I, I, I, I am the vine.

Our Lord has power to spare.
See His power everywhere.
Our Lord, give power to me.
Without Him I'm nothing, you see.

(Repeat chorus)

Our Lord can do all things.
He made the diamond in a diamond ring.
His power is great, you see.
Without Him, what would I be?

(Repeat chorus)

GOD is Our Protector

You are my hiding place; you will protect me from trouble.
Psalm 32:7

THINKIN'
2day

Sometimes when you've

had a really rough day,

you'd like to find a hiding place.

A place where no one can find you.

A safe place where you can rest. A shelter from the

storm. Maybe it's in a secret room no one knows

about. Or maybe at the top of a tree in your yard.

Everyone needs a hiding place sometimes.

Hannah Made a Promise

(Around 1070 B.C.)

Bible Story

Hannah was married to a man named Elkanah. But she was unable to have children. Other mothers teased her until she cried and could not eat. She needed a hiding place. So Hannah went to the temple and fell before the Lord and prayed. She promised the Lord that if He gave her a son, she would give the child back to Him. Eli the priest blessed her before she went home. And in time, the Lord answered her prayer. Her son Samuel was born. Hannah had found comfort in the Lord.

God was her hiding place.

The Lord is your hiding place.
With Him you can feel safe from
your enemies. You can feel secure.
He will guard and protect you.
If you are afraid, He calms you. If you are sad,
He lifts you up. When you feel like you need a safe haven,
don't run in panic. Run to your hiding place, the Lord.

for me today!

let's sing!

You Are My Hiding Place

You, You are my hiding place.
You will protect me from trouble all my days.
You, You are my hiding place.
You will protect me, Oh, my God.
Love me, hold me, touch me, comfort me.
Love me, hold me, Lord.
Touch me with Your Spirit voice.
I hear it.

(Repeat)

God is Our Shepherd

The LORD is my SHEPHERD, I shall not be in want.

Psalm 23:1

THINKIN' 2day

It was almost midnight when the group reached the river. They unloaded in a clearing next to the Appalachian Trail. The guide, Mr. Evans, said they would set up camp there. In the morning, they would begin their adventure through Newfoundland Gap. Mr. Evans had been there before. He knew the way. He had the compass and map. He would lead them. And like sheep, they would gladly follow!

David, the Shepherd Boy

(Around 1025 B.C.)

David learned how to be a shepherd when he was a small boy. He knew that sheep weren't very smart.  In fact, they were pretty goofy animals. They needed to be led or they would go the wrong way. They needed to be fed because they couldn't find a good pasture by themselves. They needed a protector who cared about them, because they couldn't defend themselves. David learned that shepherds lead the sheep, feed the sheep, and take care of the sheep.

You can read this story in 1 Samuel 17:34-37!

The Lord is like a shepherd.

He knows your needs. And if you choose to follow Him, He will lead you.

He will lead you in paths of righteousness.

A path is not a freeway. So you may not see many others walking the same way you are.

But He's the Good Shepherd.

He knows what you need and the way that is best for you!

let's sing!

The Lord Is My Shepherd

Chorus
The Lord is, the Lord is my shepherd.
The Lord is, the Lord is my shepherd.
The Lord is, the Lord is my shepherd.
How about you?
Yes He is!

The Lord is like a shepherd; He knows what to do.
The Lord is like a shepherd; He'll walk with you.
The Lord is like a shepherd; He knows what to do.
When His little lambs are tired, He'll help them through!
When His little lambs are tired, He'll help them through!

The Lord is like a shepherd; He guards my way.
The Lord is like a shepherd, watching night and day.
The Lord is like a shepherd; He guides my way,
Keeping all the enemies far away,
Keeping all the enemies far away.

God Keeps Me Safe

The name of the LORD is a strong tower; the righteous run to it and are SAFE.

Proverbs 18:10

Smoke poured from the windows of the grocery store. A crowd soon gathered, making it difficult to pass through the street. Shoppers, reporters, and concerned onlookers all pushed against one another to watch the scene unfold.

Suddenly, the crowd parted to allow one man to walk through. He didn't say a word. He didn't have to.

It read "Fire Department" across his badge, and the crowd knew he was there to help.

Esther Saved Her People

(Around 480 B.C.)

Esther knew there was great power in the name of the Lord. She knew it could demand authority even with kings! Esther, a Jew, was the queen of Persia. She discovered an evil plot by a man named Haman. He was planning to kill all of the Jews. Esther spoke to her cousin Mordecai. Mordecai called upon the name of the Lord and asked Him to help His people. Esther then asked King Xerxes to help her. Her request was granted. The name of the Lord is mighty. The Lord will help His people when they call upon Him.

You can read
the whole story
in the Book of Esther!

The name of the Lord is a gift for you.

His name can move crowds.

It can move kings. His name has great authority when you call upon God.

Situations can sometimes be very frightening, and you can be tempted to give in to pressure.

But don't let the situation change your faith. Let your faith change the situation. Because the name of the Lord is like a strong tower, you'll be safe with Him!

The Name of the Lord

Chorus
The name of the Lord is a strong tower;
The righteous run to it and are safe.
The name of the Lord is a strong tower;
The righteous run to it and are safe.
The righteous run to it and are safe.

In the Old Testament,
There is a name I love to sing.
In the Old Testament,
There is a name; life it brings.
Yahweh, my Lord,
Great and mighty You are.
Yahweh, I give You my life.
Come into my heart.

(Repeat chorus)

In the New Testament,
There is a name I love to sing.
In the New Testament,
There is a name joy it brings.
Jesus, my King,
Great and mighty You are.
Jesus, I give You my life.
Come into my heart.

(Repeat chorus)

40

GOD Plans My Future

"For I know the **PLANS** I have for you," declares the LORD.
Jeremiah 29:11

It was Maria's birthday, and no one remembered. *No cake, no candles, no party . . . how could they forget?* she wondered. Mom walked in and said, "I don't feel like cooking tonight. Let's just go to Pizza Palace to eat." When they arrived, Dad told Maria, "Go sit at that table while I order." Maria sat down and found a letter on the table with her name on it. The note inside read "Go to the play room." When Maria walked into the play room, "Surprise!" came the shouts of all her friends. "We've been planning this day for weeks!" Mom told her. "Did you really think we had forgotten your birthday?"

Jeremiah Gives Hope

(Around 627 B.C.)

Bible Story

Jeremiah once sent a very special letter to the priests and prophets of Israel who were in captivity. It was a letter from God. The Jews thought that God had forgotten about them. But Jeremiah's letter from God promised that He had not forgotten them, that He had great plans for them, and He would soon set them free. Hearing God's plan brought hope to the people.

43

Sometimes when you're most discouraged, God is planning something wonderful for you. God knows the needs in your life, and He never forgets a single prayer. At just the time you need it most —surprise!— God steps in with many surprises. He has great plans for your life!

for me today!

let's sing!

I Know the Plans I Have for You

Chorus
I know the plans I have for you,
Declares the Lord.
I know the plans I have for you,
Declares the Lord.

I will prosper you in all you do.
I will be there to guide you.
I will be a friend until the end.
You can depend on Me.

(Repeat chorus)

I will guard your way and every day.
I'll be there beside you.
I will hear your prayer; I'm always there.
You can count on Me.

(Repeat chorus)

GOD is MY Helper

"The Lord is my HELPER; I will not be afraid."

Hebrews 13:6

Everyone needs help at one time or another.

Sometimes a problem is just too big for

one person to solve. Sometimes a burden is just too

heavy to carry alone. That's when you need a helper.

Someone who loves you and cares about you.

So, what can you do when you need

help with a problem?

Daniel in the Lions' Den

(Around 539 B.C.)

Daniel had a big problem. The king had made a law that everyone had to pray to *him* and *only him.*

But Daniel would only pray to God—not to a person! When Daniel refused to pray to the king, he was thrown into a den of hungry lions. All alone, Daniel was no match for those hungry lions. But the Lord was with him. Daniel called out for help, and God shut the mouths of the lions.

Daniel was saved!

47

God loves you and cares about you
all the time. You are never out of His sight.
You are always in His hands.
So when trouble comes, remember:
you are not alone. Call on the Lord.
There is no burden too heavy for Him, no problem
He cannot solve. Problems can be big; problems can be small.
But any problem in God's hands is *no* problem at all!

for me today!

let's sing!

The Lord Is My Helper

<u>Chorus</u>
The Lord is my helper,
The Lord is my helper,
The Lord is my helper,
I will not be afraid.

(Repeat chorus)

God loves the world He made.
God loves you too!
God knows your every need.
He will help you through.

(Repeat chorus)

God hears your every prayer.
God answers too!
God leads me everywhere.
He will lead you too!

(Repeat chorus)

GOD is Trustworthy

TRUST in the LORD with all your heart and lean not on your own understanding.

Proverbs 3:5

Dylan buckled his seat belt and looked out the window. It was the biggest engine he'd ever seen. This was his first airplane ride, and he was a little nervous. "How can this thing fly? Maybe we should get off," he told his mom. She leaned out and whispered to the passing flight attendant. The attendant smiled at Dylan and said, "Come with me." He walked with the attendant to the front of the plane. The pilot turned and said, "Welcome aboard! What can I do for you, young man?" Dylan spoke up, "How does the plane fly?" The pilot answered, "It's a little hard to understand, but trust me. I'll get you there safely. Just leave it to me." That's all Dylan needed to hear!

Mary Trusts God

(Around 6 B.C.)

Mary was confused. Nothing the angel had said to her made sense. She was engaged to a man named Joseph, but they weren't married yet. How could she be having a baby? She didn't understand.

The angel said to her, "Do not be afraid, Mary, you have found favor with God. You will be with child and give birth to a Son, and you are to give Him the name Jesus" (Luke 1:30–31). That's all Mary needed to hear. She answered, "I am the Lord's servant . . . May it be to me as you have said" (Luke 1:38).

You can read the whole story in Luke 1:26–38!

The Lord is like a pilot.

And many times He simply says,

"Trust Me. This will be very hard to

understand, but I plan to get you there safely.

Just leave it to Me." Can you trust Him?

Because Mary trusted Him, a Savior was born.

Jesus would later die to free the world from sin.

You can trust Him too! Even when you do not understand,

trust Him—not your feelings. Lean on Him— not your understanding.

And know that *He* is in control—not you. That's real trust!

let's sing!

Lean Not on Your Own Understanding

Chorus
Trust in the Lord with all your heart.
Trust in the Lord with all your heart.
Trust in the Lord with all your heart,
And lean not on your own understanding.
Trust in the Lord with all your heart.
Trust in the Lord with all your heart.
Trust in the Lord with all your heart, my friend.

The Lord is like a pilot,
And many times He says,
"Trust in Me; trust in Me."
The Lord is like a pilot,
In times of greatest need,
"Trust in Me; trust in Me."

(Repeat chorus)

The Lord will be my captain.
Him I will obey.
Trust in Him; trust in Him.
The Lord will be my captain.
He'll lead me all the way.
Trust in Him; trust in Him.

(Repeat chorus)

GOD is LOVE

"For God so **LOVED** the world that he gave his one and only Son, that whoever believes in him shall not perish but have eternal life."

John 3:16

When you love somebody,

you want to make that person happy.

Giving a gift is a great way to make someone happy.

When you spend your time, money, or effort to create a

gift for someone, you show that you really care.

A gift says "I love you" in a special way.

53

God So Loved the World

(The Gospel of John was written between A.D. 80 and A.D. 90. Christ was crucified in the spring of A.D. 30.)

God said, "I love you" to the whole world. And He did it in a very special way. Your loving God, whose power has no limits, whose strength cannot be measured, your God who knows all things, gave a very special gift to you. He gave His one and only Son, Jesus, to die on the cross. Because of that gift, your sins can be forgiven and you can have eternal life!

There are many kinds of gifts, big and small. Some have great value.

God's gift to you has a greater value than anyone could ever imagine— a gift of eternal life. This gift allows you to live forever in heaven. But it came at a great cost.

It cost Jesus His life. Receive this gift with great joy. It's God's gift of love to the world—and to you!

for me today!

let's sing!

For God So Loved the World

For God so loved the world,
For God so loved the world,
For God so loved the world,
That He gave His one and only Son.

That whoever believes in Him
Shall not perish
But have everlasting life.
Whoever believes in Him
Will have it, will have it
Will have everlasting life.

(Repeat)

"He will quiet you with his love."

Zephaniah 3:17

No one thought that little baby would *ever* stop crying! She started with a whimper that turned into a whine that grew into a cry that exploded into a WAIL!

Everyone in the restaurant turned to look. *What did the baby need?* A frantic mother came running back to the table.  The mom took her baby in her arms and gave  her a long-awaited bottle. That's all the baby needed. She was really quiet after that!

Jesus Calms the Storm

(Around A.D. 28)

Bible Story

One day, the disciples needed to calm down. As they were sailing across a lake, Jesus went to sleep in the back of the boat. And as he slept, a terrible storm came upon them. The waves were so high! The disciples were afraid. They woke Jesus and shouted, "Teacher, don't You care if we drown?" (Mark 4:38).

Seeing they were afraid, He comforted them by saying to the sea, "Quiet! Be still!" (Mark 4:39). And the storm stopped! It was amazing! Even the wind and waves obey Jesus!

You can read
this story
in Mark 4:35-41!

59

Sometimes there is a storm brewing inside of you. Something is wrong.

Maybe you have a hard decision to make. Maybe your feelings have been hurt.

Maybe you've done something bad. But God can bring peace to a troubled heart. Jesus can turn all your hurts into hopes. If He can calm a wild sea, He can surely calm you! Today, ask Jesus to calm the storms in your life.

for me today!

let's sing!

He Will Quiet You

Chorus
He will quiet you, oh!
He will quiet you, oh!
He will quiet you with His love, His love!
He will quiet you, oh!
He will quiet you, oh!
He will quiet you with His love, His love!
Oh, God!

When the storm is raging inside your heart,
He can calm you; He can calm you.
When the world around you is falling apart,
He can calm the storm!

(Repeat chorus)

When you're hurt and lonely 'n ready to fall,
He can calm you; He can calm you.
When your heart is troubled, no one to call,
He can calm the storm.

GOD is Gentle

A GENTLE answer turns away wrath.

Proverbs 15:1

THINKIN' 2day

People can have different

views on the same subject. Some like the rain; some do not. Some like it cold; some like it hot.

Sometimes differences can cause tempers to flare.

If you're not careful, your disagreement can turn into

an argument.  In those times, you should be

very careful with your words. We should use

kind and gentle words, not harsh words.

61

Jesus Gave a Gentle Answer

(Around A.D. 29)

Bible Story

The religious leaders and teachers brought a woman to Jesus. She had broken the law. These leaders had angry hearts. They thought she should be killed with stones.

They asked Jesus if He thought they were doing the right thing. But Jesus answered, "If any one of you is without sin, let him be the first to throw a stone" (John 8:7). Suddenly, it got very quiet. They all walked away ashamed. Jesus' gentle answer turned them away and saved the young woman. Jesus had compassion on the woman.

You can read this story in John, chapter 8!

Sometimes, you may have disagreements with others. Even friends and family may get very angry. If this happens, it is always best to do what Jesus did. He spoke a gentle answer. Shouting unkind words at each other won't help you settle your argument. Be like Jesus. Speak a gentle word.

for me today!

let's sing!

A Gentle Answer

Chorus
A gentle answer turns away the wrath
Of those who come your way. I say,
A gentle answer calms the voice,
Stills the heart; it's heaven's choice.

A gentle word, a voice so kind
Can move a heart, change a mind.
A gentle word, a voice of love
Calms a spirit with joy because

(Repeat chorus)

A gentle voice, a word of peace,
Can calm the soul, make wars cease.
A gentle voice, a glad refrain
Is like a medicine that soothes the pain.

(Repeat chorus)

GoD's Great Name

**Glorify the LORD with me;
let us exhalt his NAME together.**

Psalm 34:3

THINKIN'
2day

The building was burning out of control.

It was then that Fireman Kevin heard a little girl

crying for help. "Help!" In an instant, Fireman Kevin

scurried up the ladder to the second-floor window and

entered the flaming bedroom. Down the ladder he came

carrying the small girl. An ambulance took Jenny to the

hospital where doctors made her well. To praise Fireman

Kevin for his heroic deed, the newspaper headline

read "Fireman Kevin is a Hero!"

65

David Glorified God

(Around 1025 B.C.)

David the shepherd boy wanted everyone to know that God was his hero! So he helped write a wonderful book it's called the Book of Psalms. In it David writes that God's name should be glorified in all the earth. That means that everywhere we go we should tell people how wonderful our God is. When we tell others about His amazing grace we share the love of Jesus. When we give God credit for all the good things that happen in our lives, we glorify our Hero, and our God!

You can read more about glorifying God in Psalm 34

People are very **different** in how they
express their love for the Lord.

Some glorify God with their service.

They may help collect food for the hungry
or empty the trash at church.

Some sing; some play games with the children.

In whatever you do, glorify the Lord
and proclaim His glory throughout the **whole earth!**

for me today!

let's sing!

Let Us Exalt His Name

Chorus
Glorify, glorify the Lord with me!
Glorify, glorify the Lord with me!
Let us exalt His name together!
Let us exalt His name forever!
Glorify, glorify the Lord with me!
Glorify the Lord, our Lord!

In everything you say, glorify the Lord!
Every night and day, glorify the Lord!
In all that you do, let His glory show through!
Oh, glorify the Lord with me!

(Repeat chorus)

GOD is Patient

Be PATIENT, bearing with one another in love.

Ephesians 4:2

Matt really didn't mean to do it.

He had one hand on the glass, one hand on the door.

But when Sparky barked and came bounding through

the door—*splash!*—milk went everywhere. Mom grabbed a

handful of paper towels and said patiently,

"It's just a little spill. It's okay."

Together Mom and Matt cleaned up the milk.

69

The Prodigal Son

(Around A.D. 28)

Jesus tells of a patient father who loved his two sons dearly. The younger one said, "Give me my share of the family inheritance now. I am leaving for a far country." The loving father did as his son had asked. The son moved away and soon wasted all of his money. He became so hungry that he took a job feeding pigs and even ate their food. One day, he came to his senses. *I'll go home and work for my father,* he thought. When he was almost home, his patient father ran to him and hugged him. The boy said, "I am no longer worthy to be called your son. May I work for you?" But his father loved him and

celebrated his return!

You can read this story in Luke, chapter 15!

A big part of loving someone is showing patience. Sometimes, you have to put up with things you don't like. No one plants a seed of corn in the ground and comes back the next day asking, "Where's the corn?" You must be patient. Good things take a little time. Today, practice a little patience with your family and friends.

for me today!

let's sing!

Be Patient

You've planted a seed in a garden today.
Be patient, for this we do know.
You've planted a seed,
Now there's coming a day.
Be patient, the flower will grow.

Chorus
Be patient, be patient,
Bearing with one another in love.
Be patient, be patient,
Be patient, the flower will grow.

You've planted a seed in the Lord's holy name.
Be patient for this we do know.
You've planted a seed.
Pray in time for the rain.
Be patient, the flower will grow.

(Repeat chorus)

GoD is GooD

Give thanks to the LORD, for he is GooD.

Psalm 136:1

The girls' gymnastics team was traveling in a small van to a competition. It was beginning to snow, when suddenly the engine began to sputter. To everyone's horror, the van just stopped. There they sat, broken down in the snow. A few minutes later, a truck driver pulled in behind the van. "Having trouble?" he asked. Then the man opened the hood, made some adjustments, and—*vrooom!*—the engine started. In all of the excitement, the team forgot to say thank you—all except Cindy. She ran back to the man's truck and said,

"Thanks, Mister!"

The Ten Lepers

(Around A.D. 30)

Bible Story

Once, Jesus was on His way to Jerusalem. He met ten men who had leprosy. They cried out, "Jesus, Master, have pity on us!" (Luke 17:13). Jesus told them to go and show themselves to the priest. As they went, they were healed! But only one of the ten men came back to thank Jesus for what He had done.

Jesus asked, "Were not all ten cleansed? Where are the other nine?" (Luke 17:17). Jesus blessed the one who said thank you.

From the time you were very small, you've probably been taught to say thank you. But do you remember to thank the most important One of all? Let God know every day how thankful you are.

Thank Him for His protection. Thank Him for the love He has shown to you. Thank Him for His goodness to you and your family. Offer a prayer of thanksgiving this very minute. He is a good God!

for me today!

let's sing!

O, Give Thanks

Chorus
O, give thanks to the Lord!
O, give thanks for He is good!
O, give thanks to the Lord!
O, give thanks for He is good!
Lift up His praises; let all the children say,
Lift up your praises to the Lord today!
O, give thanks to the Lord!
O, give thanks to the Lord!

Thank Him, thank Him, thank Him for the blue sky.
Thank Him for eyes to see the world.
Thank Him, thank Him, all you children.
Thank Him, every boy and girl!

(Repeat chorus)

Thank Him, thank Him, thank Him for Jesus Christ.
Thank Him for all He's done for you.
Thank Him, thank Him, all you children.
Thank Him, it's what all God's people do!

(Repeat chorus)

God is Our Savior

"**Everyone who calls on the name of the Lord will be saved.**"

Romans 10:13

If you saw an accident and needed to get help fast, who would you call?

Would you call the pizza delivery man? Or the plumber? Of course not! You'd call 9-1-1 and get the emergency medical team on its way. There may be days when you feel bad or sad or upset. That's when you need to remember who to call.

Call upon the Lord!

77

Our Savior Heals the Blind Man

(Around A.D. 30)

Bible Story

One day Jesus was passing through Jericho. A blind man heard the noise of the crowds and wondered what was happening. He could not see. His friends told him that Jesus had come to Jericho. The blind man knew he needed help if he was ever going to see. He shouted, "Jesus . . . have mercy on me!" (Luke 18:38). Jesus heard the blind man calling His name. Jesus answered and healed him. The blind man could see!

What a miracle! What a Savior!

You can read
this story in
Luke, chapter 18!

It is very important to know who to call when you need help. The blind man knew that only Jesus could give him sight. So, he called upon the name of the Lord. He was saved from his blindness.

You can call upon the name of the Lord and be saved from danger, bullies, temptation, and even your sin.

He will help you today. Just call on Him!

let's sing!

Everyone Who Calls on the Name of the Lord

Chorus
Everyone, everyone, everyone,
Who calls on the name of the Lord,
They will be saved forever,
Everyone who calls,
Everyone who calls,
On the name of the Lord.

When trouble comes to call,
You're just about to fall,
Call on the name of the Lord.
When people are unkind,
A friend is hard to find,
Call on the Lord.

(Repeat chorus)

When sickness comes to stay,
You need a brighter day,
Call on the name of the Lord.
When sadness fills your heart,
Tears about to start,
Call on the Lord.

(Repeat chorus)

God is Perfect

"As for God, his way is perfect; the word of the LORD is flawless."

2 Samuel 22:31

THINKIN' 2day

Ben and his dad just stared at the map, confused.

Some roads followed along the shore.

Some went to the shore and circled back into the mainland. But none went across to the tiny island.

How could they get there? "Nobody gets to the island except by the ferry," the man at the gas station told them. So Ben and his dad bought their tickets for the ten o'clock ferry, and off they went.

Sometimes, there's only one way to get there!

Jesus Is the Way

(Around A.D. 30)

Jesus once told His disciples that He was going to go and prepare a place for them. He said He would return and take them to where He was. He told them, "You know the way to the place where I am going" (John 14:4). Thomas asked,

"Lord, we don't know where you are going, so how can we know the way?"

Jesus answered, "I am the way and the truth and the life. No one comes to the Father except through me" (John 14:5–6).

You can read
this story in
John, chapter 14!

God's way isn't always the easy way,

    but it's the way to peace.

God's way isn't always the short way,

    but it's the way home. God's way isn't

always the fast way, but it is the right way.

    Jesus said, "I am the way." The only way!

If you want to know and love God, you need to follow Jesus.

for me today!

let's sing!

His Way Is Perfect

Lots of ways to go,
Lots of ways you know.
As for God, His way is perfect.
Many roads to take,
Some a big mistake.
As for God, His way is perfect.
Oh, He's waiting for you,
Waiting to show His way!
Oh, He's waiting for you,
So walk with Him today!

Chorus
As for God, His way is perfect.
As for God, His way is true.
The Word of the Lord is flawless,
So let's walk with Him, please do!

Jesus is the way
For the world today.
As for God, His way is perfect.
Detour up ahead!
Don't wanna be misled.
As for God, His way is perfect.
Oh, He's waiting for you,
Waiting to show His way!
Oh, He's waiting for you,
So walk with Him today!

(Repeat chorus)

God Works for Our Good

And we know that in all things God works for the good of those who love him.
Romans 8:28

Have you ever had to work very hard for something you wanted really badly? Practicing for a recital can be tiring! Studying for a test can be brain-bending! Learning to ride a bike can be painful! But you keep on trying because you know something good is going to come from all of that hard work. Then, when you finally play your song perfectly, ace the test, or zoom around the block on your bike, you know it was all worth it!

The Crucifixion of Jesus

(Around A.D. 30)

Jesus knew that all things work together for good—even when He was hung on the cross to die.

Although it was the saddest day ever, Jesus knew that something good was about to happen.

He knew the world would soon be rejoicing. And three days later, all things did work together for good. He arose! And the sins of all who love Him were forgiven. Jesus is always

working for our good!

You can read this story in the Gospel of Matthew, chapter 27, verse 32 through chapter 28; Mark, chapters 15 and 16; and Luke, chapters 23 and 24!

God has given a promise:

All things will work together for

the good of those who love Him.

So no matter what happens, keep trusting

in Jesus! He loves you so much that He died

to save you. He will work for the good in your life.

for me today!

let's sing!

In All Things

<u>Chorus</u>
And we know that in all things,
God works for the good of those who love Him.
And we know that in all things,
God works for the good of those who love Him.

God has given a promise,
And I know it is true.
All things are working together
For the good of those who believe. Do you?

(Repeat chorus)

God has given a promise.
I will trust in the Lord!
All things are working together
Whether good or bad. In my heart I'm sure . . .

(Repeat chorus)

Your word is a lamp to my feet and a light for my path.

Psalm 119:105

THINKIN' 2day

One summer, Lindsay visited her grandfather's farm.

After dinner each night, she and Granddad would walk

down a small path to the barn to

check on the horses. Since the

path had no lights, Granddad

would carry a lantern to light the way.

Granddad knew the way so well,

Lindsay would stay close to him and

walk in the light.

Paul on the Damascus Road

(Around A.D. 35)

The missionary Paul wasn't always a believer in Jesus Christ. In fact, before he became a Christian, his name was Saul. Saul spent his days looking for Christians so he could put  them into prison. One day as he neared Damascus, a bright light flashed around him.

Then he heard a voice saying, "Why do you persecute me?" (Acts 9:4). Saul was afraid and asked, "Who are you?" The voice answered, "I am Jesus" (Acts 9:5–6). Saul was blinded by the bright light. But three days later, he could see once again.

When Saul became a Christian, his name was changed to Paul. He taught many people about Jesus.

You can read
the whole story
in Acts, chapter 9!

God's Word is like a lamp. It allows you to see clearly the things ahead. Without a lamp, you might stumble and fall. You may wonder what tomorrow might bring. But don't worry, God has that under control. Just stay close to your Father by praying, obeying, and studying the Bible. And step into God's light!

for me today!

let's sing!

Your Word Is a Lamp

Chorus
Your word is a lamp to my feet
And a light for my path.
Wherever I am going,
Your word is a lamp to my feet
And a light for my path,
Wherever I go.

Just like a candle in the darkness,
You show me the way to go.
Just like a candle in the darkness,
You brighten my life, I know.

(Repeat chorus)

Just like a candle in the darkness,
I can see all around me there.
Just like a candle in the darkness,
You're leading me everywhere.

(Repeat chorus)